Are Humans Causing
CLIMATE CHANGE?

By Naomi Osborne

KidHaven
PUBLISHING

Published in 2020 by
KidHaven Publishing, an Imprint of Greenhaven Publishing, LLC
353 3rd Avenue
Suite 255
New York, NY 10010

Designer: Deanna Paternostro
Editor: Vanessa Oswald

Photo credits: Cover, p. 7 FloridaStock/Shutterstock.com; p. 5 (top) Galyna Andrushko/Shutterstock.com; p. 5 (bottom) Tatiana Grozetskaya/Shutterstock.com; p. 9 Kitnha/Shutterstock.com; p. 11 Alexis Rosenfeld/Getty Images; p. 13 Robert Crum/Shutterstock.com; p. 15 (background) Roschetzky Photography/Shutterstock.com; p. 15 (inset) Designua/Shutterstock.com; p. 17 (top) Daily Herald Archive/SSPL/Getty Images; p. 17 (bottom) Robyn Beck/AFP/Getty Images; p. 19 KPG Payless2/Shutterstock.com; p. 21 (notepad) ESB Professional/Shutterstock.com; p. 21 (markers) Kucher Serhii/Shutterstock.com; p. 21 (photo frame) FARBAI/iStock/Thinkstock; p. 21 (inset, left) Olivier Le Queinec/Shutterstock.com; p. 21 (inset, middle-left) CherylRamalho/Shutterstock.com; p. 21 (inset, middle-right) Ankor Light/Shutterstock.com; p. 21 (inset, right) Rich Carey/Shutterstock.com.

Cataloging-in-Publication Data

Names: Osborne, Naomi.
Title: Are humans causing climate change? / Naomi Osborne.
Description: New York : KidHaven Publishing, 2020. | Series: Points of view | Includes glossary and index.
Identifiers: ISBN 9781534532083 (pbk.) | ISBN 9781534531963 (library bound) | ISBN 9781534532144 (6 pack) | ISBN 9781534532021 (ebook)
Subjects: LCSH: Climatic changes–Juvenile literature. | Climatic changes–Effect of human beings on–Juvenile literature. | Climatic changes–Government policy–Juvenile literature. | Global warming--Juvenile literature.
Classification: LCC QC903.15 O83 2020 | DDC 363.738'74–dc23

Printed in the United States of America

CPSIA compliance information: Batch #BW20KL: For further information contact Greenhaven Publishing LLC, New York, New York at 1-844-317-7404.

Please visit our website, www.greenhavenpublishing.com. For a free color catalog of all our high-quality books, call toll free 1-844-317-7404 or fax 1-844-317-7405.

CONTENTS

Different
VIEWPOINTS

Change in the weather over a long period of time is known as climate change. Some people believe humans are causing climate change by causing global warming, which is the state of Earth getting hotter. Although scientists have facts to support this, there are some people who are **skeptical** of these facts and think something else may be causing climate change.

Both sides of the **debate** on climate change feel strongly about their different points of view. Even though people may not agree, hearing each other's opinions can be helpful in learning more about such an important topic.

Know the Facts!

The year 2016 was the warmest year since 1880, according to the National Aeronautics and Space Administration (NASA).

Many scientists say there are plenty of things humans do that cause climate change. However, not everyone believes this claim. Learning about both sides of any argument is important in order to have an informed, or educated, opinion on a subject.

CLIMATE

In the last century, the earth has warmed up by 1.8°F (1°C). This rise in temperature has changed the weather and climate in different places. Weather is the minute-by-minute changes in the air, or the atmosphere, on our planet. Climate is what the weather is like over a long time in an area.

These changes in weather and climate can **damage** the **habitats** of humans, animals, plants, and other creatures, making it harder for them to live. Some changes brought on by global warming include more rainfall, shrinking sea ice, flooding, and droughts.

Know the Facts!

It's not correct to say that global warming can't be real because winters are colder. Global warming can lead to hotter summers and colder winters.

The shrinking sea ice in the Arctic **affects** polar bears' habitats.

A Combination
OF CAUSES

While many scientists say humans are the main cause of climate change, there are some scientists who disagree. They often believe a combination of human activity and natural changes is leading to climate change. Others say there isn't enough **information** to make the claim that only humans are responsible.

These scientists argue that Earth's climate has gone through periods of warming and cooling throughout the centuries. They believe the rise in temperature in the 20th and 21st centuries is in line with natural temperature changes over the past 3,000 years.

Know the Facts!

Scientists have been debating whether humans cause global warming since the late 19th century.

Some scientists believe global warming isn't
caused by humans, but instead is caused by constant changes in
ocean currents—shown here—and the sun's heat.

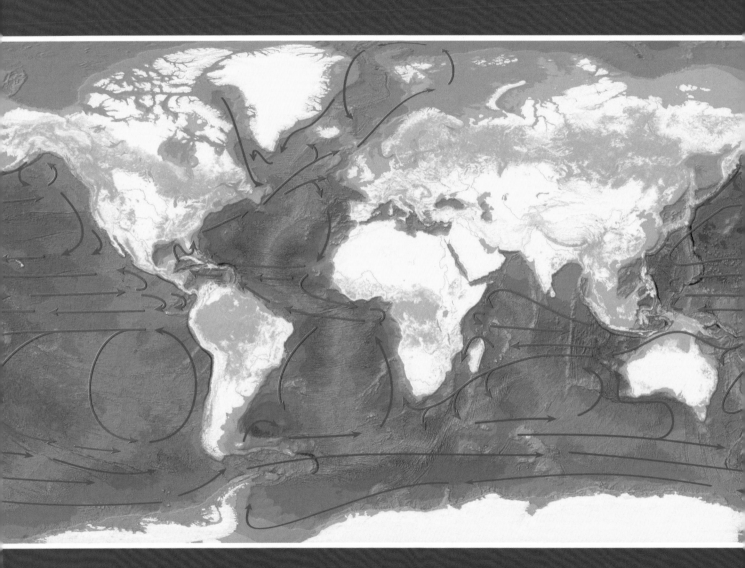

Rising
TEMPERATURES

According to scientists who study climate change, the global temperature is quickly rising. This sharp increase in the warming of Earth has taken place in the last 35 years. The five warmest years recorded have all happened since 2010.

Several studies claim that 97 percent or more of climate scientists agree that global warming, which they believe is caused by humans, is the direct cause of climate change. Scientists believe this increase in temperature is too much too fast to be purely natural. They believe human activity is causing big problems for the earth!

Know the Facts!

When the corals that make up coral reefs get too hot, they **shed** the algae—plantlike creatures—living on them, making them turn white. This is called "coral bleaching," which is caused by global warming.

Scientists believe the effects of human activity on Earth can be seen in changes to the climate, the air, and the oceans. Coral bleaching—shown here—is a sign of global warming.

SUSTAINABILITY

Some leaders have argued that average people are being affected in harmful ways by the belief that humans are the only cause of climate change. For example, the price of **sustainable** products, such as solar panels, can be expensive for homeowners.

Jobs are also being lost because of the movement away from **fossil fuels**. Many people don't think the burning of fossil fuels is enough of a problem to **justify** people losing their jobs. They argue that the efforts to deal with climate change are hurting people more than climate change at this point.

Know the Facts!

In 2019, an average solar panel system in the United States cost $12,810. Solar panels change energy from the sun into electricity people can use in their homes.

Solar panels and other sustainable products cost a lot of money.

Greenhouse
EFFECT

Many scientists claim the burning of fossil fuels by humans causes climate change. They're nonrenewable resources, which means they take millions of years to form and more can't be made quickly enough to be used by all those who need them.

The burning of fossil fuels creates **air pollution** and puts greenhouse gases such as carbon dioxide into the air. These gases create a kind of blanket around the earth that traps heat from the sun and keeps it from escaping. This warming of the earth is called the "greenhouse effect" because the gases trap heat like the glass in a greenhouse.

Know the Facts!

Humans use fossil fuels daily. They power cars, provide heat and electricity in our homes, and are used in factories to run machines. Fossil fuels are also used to make some plastics, makeup, and drugs.

Many factories burn fossil fuels, which puts greenhouse gases into the air. Scientists believe the greenhouse effect has led to climate change.

greenhouse effect

The Effect of
EMISSIONS

Many people agree that greenhouse gases harm the earth, but some don't believe they're a major reason for climate change. They claim the **emissions** given off are too small to change the climate. Their argument is that the earth can handle a certain amount of these gas emissions as it has for centuries.

Some scientists also say a lot of the greenhouse gases, such as carbon dioxide, put into the atmosphere are **absorbed** by carbon sinks, which are things in nature that suck up and store carbon dioxide. Some of these carbon sinks include plants, trees, oceans, and soil.

Know the Facts!

Plants go through photosynthesis to make energy to live and grow. Sunlight, water, minerals, and carbon dioxide are absorbed and used to make food for the plant. Oxygen is then produced by the plant and is put into the air.

Some people argue that humans are causing less damage to the earth now than they did when there were fewer rules in place for factories.

DEFORESTATION

Trees absorb carbon dioxide, a greenhouse gas, and release, or put, oxygen into the air. However, when trees are cut down, they can no longer absorb carbon dioxide. If trees are burned by people, the carbon dioxide is released back into the atmosphere, which might lead to climate change.

Forests are cut down for wood or to make room for farms, roads, and other spaces for people to use. The loss of these forests, which is called deforestation, can affect wildlife, weather patterns, and the climate in different areas.

Know the Facts!

More than 200,000 acres (80,937 ha) of rain forest are burned every day. This means there are more than 150 acres (60.7 ha) lost every minute and 78 million acres (31,565,480 ha) lost every year!

Deforestation has been connected to climate change.

POINT OF VIEW?

People have many different points of view when it comes to the causes of climate change, so it's important to form your own opinion based on **reputable** sources on the subject. It's also good to learn about all sides of the debate.

Even though people may have a different point of view than you, it's important to respect their right to have their own opinion and to understand why they feel the way they do about a topic. Based on the different facts and points of view you have read, do you think humans cause climate change?

Know the Facts!

Some celebrities fighting climate change include Emma Thompson, Jane Fonda, Brad Pitt, and Leonardo DiCaprio.

Are humans causing climate change?

YES

- Most scientists agree that humans are a main cause of global warming, which is causing climate change. The temperature on Earth has risen too quickly to be caused by nature alone.

- Burning fossil fuels produces greenhouse gases, which trap heat on Earth and cause temperatures to rise.

- When humans cut down trees, there are fewer plants to take in carbon dioxide, which makes global warming worse.

NO

- Climate change is a natural part of Earth's history.

- The human connection to climate change isn't strong enough to support the loss of jobs and the costs that come with trying to deal with this problem.

- Greenhouse gases are part of natural processes on Earth, and carbon sinks absorb some of these gases.

You can use a chart such as this one to see both sides of the debate on whether humans cause climate change and then form your own opinion.

GLOSSARY

absorb: To soak up.

affect: To produce an effect on something.

air pollution: Solid particles and gases in the air that are harmful.

damage: To cause harm. Also, harm done to something.

debate: An argument or discussion about an issue, generally between two sides.

emission: A gas that is sent out or given off.

fossil fuel: A fuel, such as coal, oil, or natural gas, that is formed in the earth from dead plants or animals.

habitat: A living space for an animal, plant, or human.

information: Knowledge or facts about something.

justify: To show or prove to be right.

reputable: Able to be trusted.

shed: To get rid of.

skeptical: Likely to question something.

sustainable: Able to last for a long time without doing much damage to nature.

For More
INFORMATION

WEBSITES

NASA: Climate Kids

climatekids.nasa.gov/climate-change-meaning/
This website gives a clear definition of climate change and provides several facts on the subject.

National Geographic Kids: What Is Climate Change?

www.natgeokids.com/au/discover/geography/general-geography/what-is-climate-change/
This website offers information on climate change and its many causes, from burning fossil fuels to deforestation.

BOOKS

Duling, Kaitlyn. *Rising Temperatures*. New York, NY: Cavendish Square, 2019.

Howell, Izzi. *Energy Eco Facts*. New York, NY: Crabtree Publishing Company, 2019.

Shoals, James. *What Is Climate Change?*. Broomall, PA: Mason Crest, 2020.

Publisher's note to educators and parents: Our editors have carefully reviewed these websites to ensure that they are suitable for students. Many websites change frequently, however, and we cannot guarantee that a site's future contents will continue to meet our high standards of quality and educational value. Be advised that students should be closely supervised whenever they access the Internet.

INDEX